THE LEAST THAT I CAN DO
IS LOVE YOU.

PRAISE!

Marcus Amaker is a poet committed to living abundantly on this earth. These are big-hearted poems, rich with sound and story, enlivened by metaphor and magic. In "Why I Write Poems," his speaker says, "a sharp turn of phrase / can sting like the edge of a blunt piece of paper." This book both stings and heals.
– ***Beth Ann Fennelly*** *(she/her), poet laureate of Mississippi, 2016–21*

Hold What Makes You Whole is a gratifying meditative collection of poems accompanied by kaleidoscopic visual imagery that pulls you in, settles your mind, and makes way for one's own reflections. A journey of words through the micro and macro elements of a life. Amaker has created a collection made perfectly for this moment in time.
– ***Lisa Willis*** *(she/her), executive director of Cave Canem Foundation*

Dedicated to his great-great aunt Ruth, *Hold What Makes You Whole* is a celebration of the ways we each contain all the elements in the universe. From our families and our home place to the larger sweep of history, Marcus reminds us about the things that make us whole. Sprinkling wisdom on every page, he reminds us that "joy doesn't have / to go far / to find a home." For Marcus Amaker, "writing a poem is world building," and the worlds he brings us in this glorious collage of text and image is one where "You are free / to find heaven / even if / you don't believe / heaven exits," This book is a gift for all of us.
– ***Marjory Wentworth*** *(she/her), poet laureate of South Carolina, 2003–21*

In *Hold What Makes You Whole*, Marcus Amaker harnesses the slick and psychic echoes that our living creates. His handling of this mastery turns up an awareness of how choral and connected a self can be – across spaces, across times, across realities. And that whelming possibility is at the core of this poet's grace, because, as Amaker hears it, "what could be / more spiritual / than realizing / your spirit / has outgrown / the body / it was given?" Bless this book.
– ***Geffrey Davis** (he/him), author of "Night Angler"*
(BOA Editions)

One of the most multitalented poets in the country, Amaker turns his eye and ear to the body in his new collection, *Hold What Makes You Whole.* Combining poems, photography, and illustration, Amaker asks big questions of the vessels that carry us through life: How do our bodies hold grief? Identity? Loved ones? How is it that "My eyes are closed / and I can / still see you?" How can the exhaustion of fatherhood make one's eyelids "heavy with daylight?" "I've come to be in bloom," Amaker says, and for him, the flower has many kinds of petals. Conducting his way through a symphony in which he is also the instruments, Amaker harmonizes words with images with handwriting with typography. "Everything that has wings is kinfolk," he says, and everything Amaker touches in this beautiful book begins to fly.
– ***P. Scott Cunningham** (he/him), founder/director,*
O, Miami Poetry Festival

HOLD WHAT MAKES YOU WHOLE

FREE VERSE PRESS
A FREE VERSE, LLC EXPERIENCE

a s

e is a safe haven for geese
to gather.
it's the wood carp
hanging
on the wall.
The of striped blues
of carpet patterns,
color
the pschedelic colors of
kid toys,
spilling over on a
floor that is
covered in cat hair and
inevitable dust.

ome is the sound of my
daughters voice, her shoes
a instr
a percussive
out of the hardwood floor,
it is the clicking of the record
player to 45, to the
crunchy guitar riff of an all-female
the morn

BOOKS BY MARCUS AMAKER

Listening To Static (2005)
Poems For Augustine (2005)
The Soft Paper Cut (2007)
The Present Presence (2012)
The Spoken Word. Selected Poems: 2003–13 (2013)
Mantra: An Interactive Poetry Book (2015)
Empath (2017)
The Birth of All Things (2020)
Black Music Is (2021)

As an editor

Colors Wash Over Me: Poems by Lowcountry Students, Volume One (2021–22) (2022)
I Am a Furious Wish: Anthology of Lowcountry Poets, Volume One (2022)

MUSIC BY MARCUS AMAKER

Big Butt (1986)
Gimme Some (1987)
Play It (1988)
Say No! (1988)
Daydreamin' (1988)
All Uv the Time (1989)
The New Foundation (with Quentin E. Baxter) (2014)
Empath (with Quentin E. Baxter) (2018)
Muscle Memory (with Quentin E. Baxter) (2021)
ELECTROPOEMS (2022)

As tape loop
Minimalism (2005)
Dealate (2005)
Escapism (2006)
1945 (2008)
Lady Phoenix (2009)
Digital Detox (2010)
The Cassette Demos (2011)
Sunday Rain (2011)
Animation (2012)
The Drum Machine, Part 1 (2015)
Analogue // 1–6 (2016–17)
Telemaque. (2017)
Open (2018)
Empath (Variations) (2018)
Creating Empty Space (2019)
The Birth of All Things (2019)
The Weight That Holds the Animal (2019)
Rei (2019)
Contagion (2020)
Rhythm Vaccine (2020)
subversive (2020)
TEXTURE // 1 (with Concept RXCH) (2021)
kept & let go of (2022)
flushed & in bloom (2022)

tapeloop.bandcamp.com

The author is available for performances and writing workshops.
If interested, please email **marcus@marcusamaker.com.**

Paperback ISBN: 978-1-7346737-2-2
E-book ISBN: 978-1-7374696-7-4
Audiobook ISBN: 978-1-7374696-8-1

Library of Congress Control Number: 2022948776

Front cover image and Ruth Robinson photos
courtesy of Lynn R. Miller
Family photos courtesy of Betty & Willie Amaker
Back cover author photo by Diana Deaver
Inside author photo courtesy of Palmetto Bluff
Edited by Stacy Chandler
Book design and layout by Marcus Amaker
Dried leaf images by Anastezia Luneva

Printed in the United States of America.
First printing edition 2023.

Published by Free Verse Press
Free Verse, LLC
North Charleston, South Carolina
freeversepress.com

DEDICATION

This book is for **Ruth Hubbard Robinson** (1926–2020), my great-great aunt. She's on the cover of this collection. Ruth published her first and only book of poetry, *IMAGES: Mirrored from the Heart,* when she was 65. She was a community activist, friend, mother, and quilter. We had regular phone conversations when she was in her 90s. She believed in my work intimately and beautfully.

Our plan was to edit and republish her book after the worst of COVID was over. She transitioned before that could happen. My plan is to get the book done for you, Aunt Ruth.

Readers, it's my honor to introduce you to her Spirit.

TRACKLIST

TRACKLIST

TRACKLIST

TRACKLIST

HOLD WHAT MAKES
YOU WHOLE

OF COLOR

When someone asks you
why it hurts the earth
to pull one flower
from a field of flowers,
tell them you are the lilac
or the hibiscus,
growing and sunbathing
in a community of natural color,
and you know a lot of kinfolk
who have the same roots. Tell them
your kind of people are earth
people, and if there's anything
you know, it's the pain of one
of your petals being picked,
of your homelife disrupted by
fires, bugs, concrete, or men
who are too distracted by what's
above them. Men who are too focused
on skylines to notice their dirty shoes
walking on sacred ground.
So, yes – when one of us is uprooted
or displaced from the soil
that raised us, we feel it. Tell them,
"You would feel it,
too – especially if the flower
looked like you, or was
anywhere close to the
same hue."

CONNECTING THE DOTS

I've never been able to remember the
names of constellations. My eyes
have seen many stars, but none of
them have left an
impression that lasts longer

than the time it takes to blink
them away. All they do is
shine from a distance.

Shine as if being bright
is enough light to survive
in a heavy & dark
experience. Besides, they only

come out at night, and I am a
creature of the sun.

But then, NASA shares a photo of
galaxies, and I instantly
feel connected to it all.

I am small.

A speck of stardust trying to
remember what life was like
without time. Before
someone told me that it
was illegal to go out of my

mind. Before someone made
me believe that I am
separate from anything. But I am
the atmosphere.
I am time.

I am everything that I don't
understand. I am a catalog
of moments sprinkled
with memory.

I am the constellation
That's shaped like a snake.

Orion's killer. But I am not a
murderer;

just a Scorpio
with a sharp tongue who
sometimes wonders if
his eyesight is good enough

to see when an imminent path
has been set ablaze.

I want to hold people closer than the stars
hold our attention.
I want to admire them for
longer than a

firework spark.

I want to be the fiery friend who
chooses to be charged up
after every electric
conversation.

As far as I know, we can't hold
stars in our hands, but
ecstasy glows

and cradles
us with its
absolute power,

encouraging us to look up
and see through the story of
ourselves as people. See
through the story of
ourselves as anything less

than celestial bodies
surging toward

nirvana.

simply walking outside
I was drowning in
own
cold
shadow

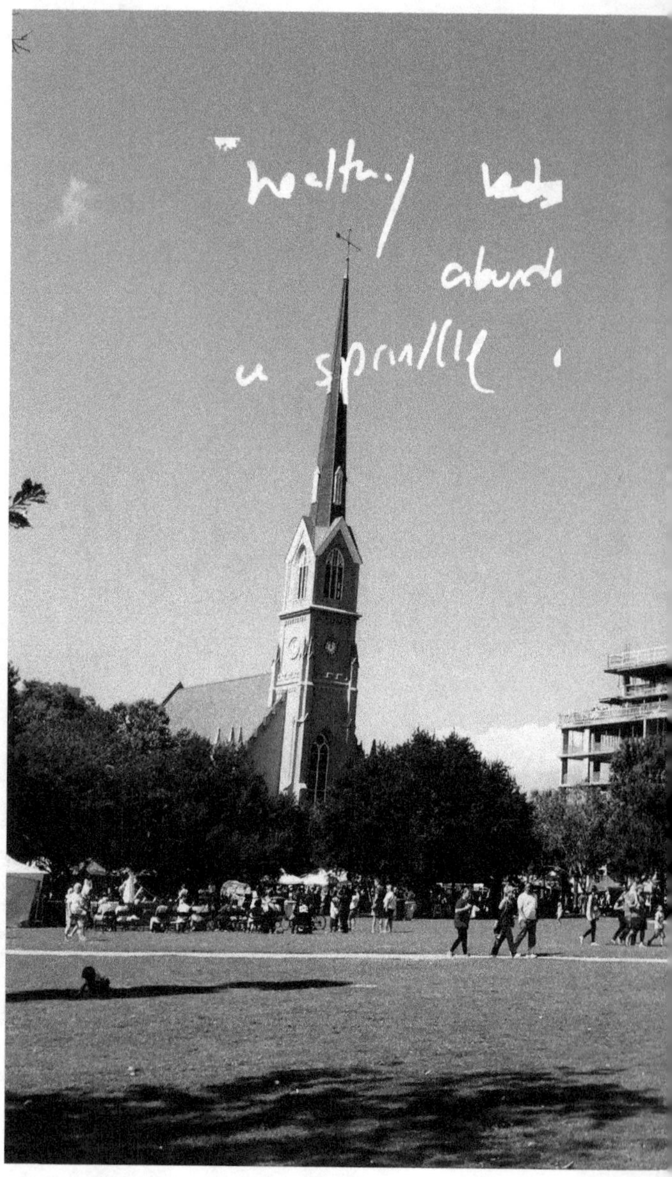

WHY I WRITE POEMS

Because I can't say my last name
to a stranger without stuttering.
Because written words will age
and change tone with time.
Because my speaking voice will
eventually go silent.
Because my pen is as dark as my mind.
Because when there's a gnat in my cocktail
I wonder if it had a death wish.
Because I think about the history
and intention of insects.
Because I wonder if house keys
go into hiding on purpose.
Because sometimes I, too, want to
stay secluded when I am lost.
Because poetry opens doors.
Because writing a poem is world building.
Because it insists I work on the things
I've been resisting.
Because a sharp turn of phrase
can sting like the edge of a blunt piece of paper.

BACTERIA

Someone told me
that all life
evolved from
an organism
with a single
cell.

I told them
that racism
is mutating
and will lock us
back into
one.

THEY / THEM / US

The preacher
reminds us
that we are
never truly
in our bodies.

The skin
is a blanket
for an already
warm soul,

deep sleeping
through life
before
heaven's alarm
clock. So, really,

what could be
more spiritual
than realizing
your spirit
has outgrown
the body
it was given?

What could be
more truthful
than knowing

your true self
is wide awake
in a sleeping
world?

You are free
to find heaven
even if
you don't believe
heaven exists,

you are already
the God that
God
intended.

PAPERWEIGHTS

Sorrow can appear
out of the blue
like one of those
post office
street mailboxes.

All of a sudden
it's there:

Steady as a mental road block,
sending you messages
from another time.

You thought you stamped
your worries away,
but they always come back
return to sender.

And you allow
the sadness back
inside the home
of your body
after realizing
you cannot erase
permanent ink,

you can't ignore
memories that sting
sharper than
a paper cut.

:::::::

Grief is the car
that trails you
when you are
running low on energy
and almost out of gas.

It follows you
from behind
and eventually
finds its way
into the front
of your mind,
inside your room,

and everywhere
you turn.

:::::::

Pain is in the
trauma-sparked tears
of my mother's
memory-sharp eyes
when talking about
the white girl
who, after bumping into

my mom when
she was a kid,
thought it was
dirty and disgusting
to touch brown skin.

:::::::

Heartbreak is the animal hair
you find on socks
after your cat died.

It's knowing that
you'd rather
cradle cold paws
and cross the
rainbow bridge together
than float
to heaven alone.

:::::::

Misery is the door
that stays locked
despite the fact
you built the room
and sharpened the blade
that cut the key.

:::::::

Hopelessness is the
untied shoestring
on a walk
against the wind.

It's the trip
that drowns you in despair
before folding poems
in an envelope
you mail to yourself,

kneeling
in the melancholy
of your own
mourning

and fastening
an emotion
that grips you,
grounds you
and won't
let go.

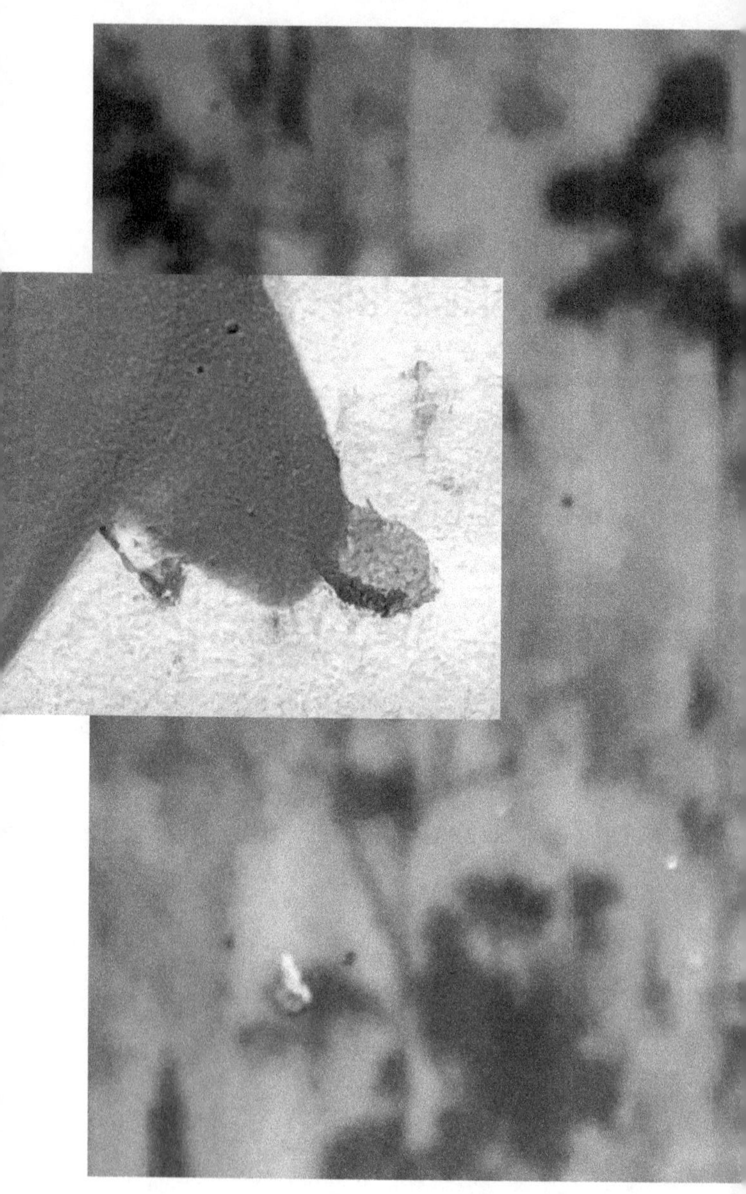

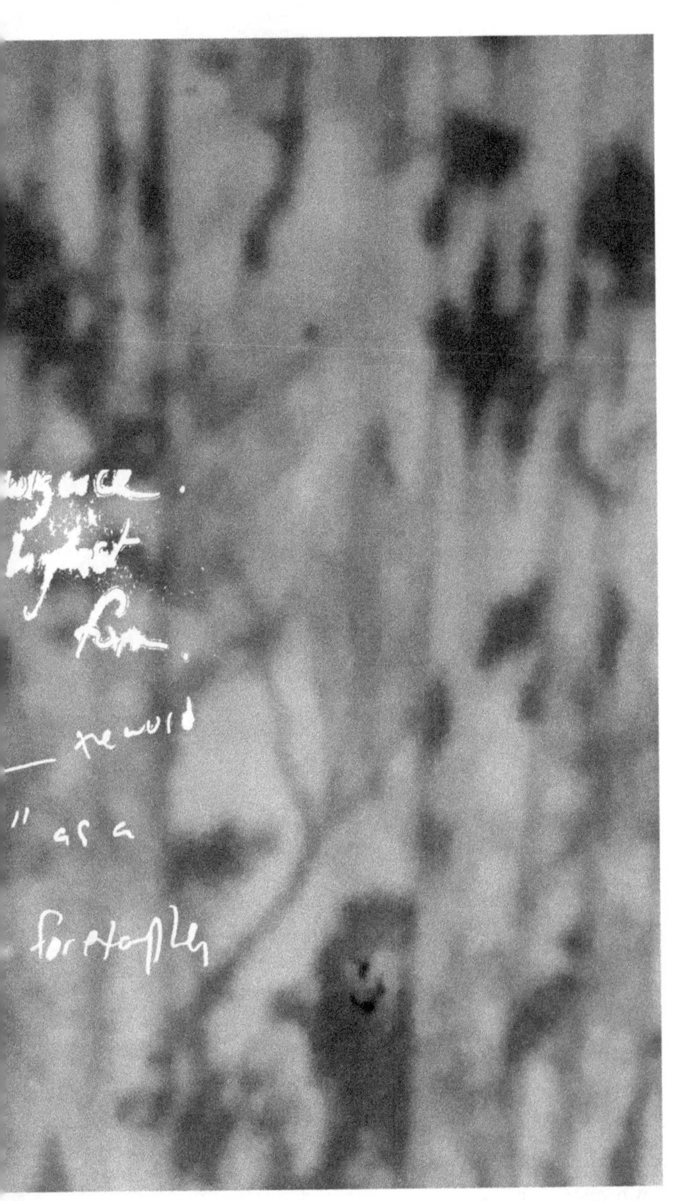
form.
the world
as a

GIVE YOURSELF SOME FLOWERS

And in the beginning,
God gave your body
a checklist:

Keep your heart
on beat
and your lungs
dancing with oxygen,
not passive to air.

Make sure
the path of your blood
slows down
for checkpoints
and avoids
bumps
in the road.

Train your nerves
to keep a balanced pace
and stay within
the lines
of steady flow.

Push forward
without putting
too much
pressure
on movement.

Remember
to return to water
when your spirit
and its frame
are in drought.

Treat your body
like a well-rounded planet
built for all seasons,

or pretend you are
an adaptable star:

Float in the black
and stay there
if you need to,

save some light
for yourself.

In other words,
rest like the sun does:

Schedule some time
to stay out of sight
when too many people
praise warm energy.

Keep in mind
all of these things

when depression
tells you
nothing is working.

Keep in mind
all of these things

when it tells you
there is no
invisible force
connecting us,

when your veins
are stopped by blood clots,

when your bones are dry,
and the water
is too quick to boil.

Keep in mind
all of these things

when it tells you
that the soul is like the body:

Made to be broken,
open to deterioration
and doubt. Yes,

keep in mind
all of these things
and remember:

Even when it
seems like
the clock isn't ticking,

you were made perfectly
for this moment
in time.

THE CREEPY CRAWLIES

for Jamal Sutherland

Cops hide behind
the bushes of busy highways
like cockroaches
planting themselves
in the shadow pathways
of your home.

Danger has an ego.

It disguises itself
in comfort,
shifts restlessly in the folds,
and waits for acknowledgement.

Lights on.

Antennas up.

Instantly, you realize
you don't have the privilege
of not being fearful.

Immediately,
you sit up straight
and your palms
start sweating.

Clutching the
now slip-stained handle
of a steering wheel
as you try to remember
how much weight
your foot can hold,

how many times
you've slammed
your shoes to the floor,

how easy it is
to confront death.

Instead of you
killing the bug,
the bug kills you.

And all of this murder
reminds you
of when you were young
and the Bible told you
"thou shall not kill."

Thou shall not kill,
I guess,
unless it is a mosquito

on your baby's forehead:

The flight of thin wings
resting after
a wind-weary
search for flesh.

In that moment,
you become executioner:

A quick palm smack
brings oblivion, or bardo,
but no blood guilt
or mercy.

Just death.

Thou shall not kill,
I guess,
unless it is that cockroach –
the bug laureate –
its slick brown skin
soon to stain
clean wall paint.

The larger the body,
the more brutal the murder.

Be it a sneaker
or poison
shot straight into the eyes.

No blood guilt
or mercy.

Just death.

And thou shall not kill,
I guess,
unless you are a policeman
and the slick brown skin
that scares you
belongs to a Black body,
still breathing
before you become slayer.

No blood guilt
or mercy.

Just death.

POINT OF VIEW

According to my daughter,
a mosquito is a hummingbird.
& everything that has wings is kinfolk.
Especially airplanes. In her mind,
a banana is a yellow moon.
A small, green acorn
is a turtle. & every object within view
should be rewarded with praise. In
our house,

we hug incense smoke
and tickle the plants.
We pull the color out of language
and make rainbow-like chatter.
She reminds me that all living things
have the right to experience laughter.

According to my daughter,
the number 5 is also an S.
The letter B is the number 8 with
a backbone. Cat ears are flower petals.
Opening a book is also opening a door.
& we make drums out of every hard
surface. Motivate melody and mischief
to flirt with the quiet. She gets up and
dances after throwing her body on the floor,

because all of it is a song.

1913

1/25/193

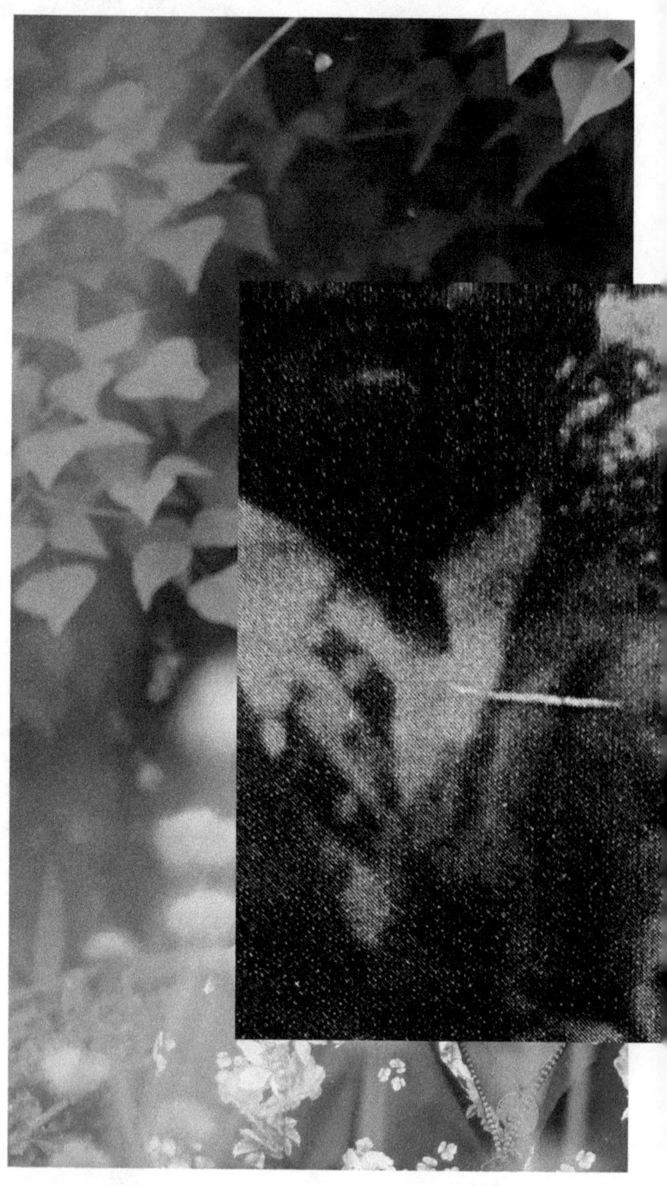

UP

Go outside
at 4:44am
and point a
flashlight
to the sky.
Use the
moment
as a reminder
that it only
takes a few steps
to unsee the walls,
vanish the ceiling,
and dissolve
the boundaries
around you.
Your light
is in constant
elevation.
All you
have to do
is turn it on.

THE WORD "SUPREME" HAS BEEN CANCELED

"Supreme" has been used to describe many
things. Most of them are divine. Oh, the divine
John Coltrane, whose *A Love Supreme* was

the ultimate example of gentle jazz syncopation.
Later, The Supremes: A perfect name for three
divine Black women who broke the sound

barrier for Motown, singing protest songs
with a smile. "Supreme" meant excellence.
Abundance in its highest form. But now,

when my daughter hears that word, it is a
form of fear and control. White supremacy
and The Supreme Court. How did the word

lose its integrity? Will other words, like "trust,"
"love," and "freedom" be overturned? I want her
to know that freedom of choice is not out of

context in the land of the "free." I demand that
her life be a part of its history. I need her to
trust the definition of words like I trust Diana

Ross to sing the truth. I want my daughter to
know that she is supreme. And divine. I want
to protect her from things that feed on
manipulation and domination. I am a powerless

parent in a broken political system. But I still want my daughter to know the word "revolution" before it, too, is taken away.

DOLLY SAID NO TO ELVIS AND YES TO WHITNEY

Because
"I Will Always Love You"
needed more
than a
swiveling hip shake
song and dance.

Because
Whitney's voice
is worth more
than Graceland.

Because
Whitney had a way
of making you
taste caramel
when a song
was already
ear candy sweet.

Because
Dolly knew
that Love,
when sung
by a Black woman,
is immortal.

Because
Elvis
wouldn't have hit
that high note
anyway.

ANOTHER POEM ABOUT STUTTERING

My voice box is a record player
stuck
on a loop / locked inside
a soundproof room. /
Sometimes

I am the only one
who hears
the dense echo
of my vibrato, / and other times

I open my mouth

and everyone around me knows

that my tongue
is a muscle too weak
to lift the weight
of sound.

////////

When I was

younger, a speech therapist
told me the key to unlocking
the melody
was in my mind / but I told him

that depression is tone deaf /

and there is no way to move the
needle without
hearing a rhythmic negative
voice
spinning inside my head.

////////

I've always believed

that conversation is not
the best way to interact
with sound, and the

people who hold on to silence
the longest
are the ones who can hear

God. /

That's why it's my
intention to
build a community
with the quiet. / To take off

my headphones and hear

heart-focused interaction

in stereo.

////////

My speaking voice

is not my thinking voice
is not my poet voice. / If

I can't say my name
when I'm around you,
it's not because I don't believe

in its power, /

it's because I tripped on the chord
on the way to the microphone.

////////

I used to think I needed
a power cord to be turned on,

I used to obsess over the dust
that scratches my throat,

I used to not know that any
noise I make is pure human

sound,

and I am not a broken record.

////////

Repeat after me:

You are
not
a broken

record.

close like
at
in

OPEN SOURCE

I want to trust the image
in the bathroom mirror like

I trust a QR code. I want to
know that my face holds

information and my body
has somewhere to go. I want to

follow where they take me. I
want my smile to be someone's

destination or an invitation to
learn more. I want to know

that every grey hair on my chin
is storing memory information.

And every mark on my skin is
exactly where it is supposed to be.

I want to scan my eyes and find
God. I want to be okay if God

doesn't look like me. I want to
hold up my phone for a selfie

and take a picture of my crush.

HONOR CODE (EMBERS)

Commissioned poem by The Citadel, a military college in South Carolina.

"If you want to lean on a tree, first make sure it can hold you."
– African proverb

Class of 1973. The only Black band member has
to learn the melody of "Dixie" and play it under a

confederate flag. Any other song would sound too
much like freedom. Survival is the ring of history's

dust chords. No harmony. Later, he was expelled
from the band and called a "radical" for wanting the

institution to change its tune; for wanting to take
a deeper breath.

Class of 1982. A young cadet dances with white
females after being called a nigger as he walked

into a party. An accomplished athlete on the
football field, a daredevil on the dance floor.

Shaking your hips takes a different kind of strength
than gridiron muscle. When accused of forgery,

he defends himself from expulsion. "To be judged
as good, I had to perform twice as good," he said.

Power tackles a new body, then scores. He calls it
the toughest challenge he's ever faced, and still

thanks God for the experience, and his breath.

Class of 1990. Five white cadets in white sheets
disrupt a 17-year-old Black man's sleep in the

middle of the night. Devils as classmates.
Cone-head cowards with no class. Shadow

confederates, still firing shots from a lost
war. A burned paper cross, permanent scars,

and a deep singe of heartbreak were left
behind. Too much smoke and trauma for a
young freshman to find clean breath.

Class of 2020. Cadets march on ashes from
dead flames. Charleston is named "The best

city in the United States" for 8 years in a row
as still-smouldering sparks shed low phantom

clouds. Somewhere, Black alumni know what
once was too hot to touch will eventually cool,

but blistered fingers will hold hands with
the body of a brotherhood still learning

how to breathe.

HEAVENLY NOSTALGIA

Maybe we actually start from dust.

Particles of some heavenly universe
before we form flesh
and are forced to adjust.

Coming in loud, full of raw emotion
into a world that hears the volume of our

vibration then tells us to hush
and quiet the noise that attached itself
to body and skin.

This is how we all begin
before brushing off the magic that
initiated from space.

But when I look into your eyes through the deep
miraculous mirror of your face,

I remember that we are born
with the black nostalgia
of planets.

Thrust into a blue horizon of water
and flesh – a steady see-saw
of life and death,

through never-ending
rhythms of parallel breath,

held by the spirit hands
of ancestors who

passed the test.

Until we return to an avalon memory.

A flickering sound of echo energy,
as wide as the shadow that
blankets every night,

spiraling up from a world

that wanted us
to be afraid of heights.

KEPT & LET GO OF

I've obsessed over so many things that eventually
ended up in a landfill. Like the fancy lamp light

that never quite turned on, and the overpriced
headphones that broke after I forced them to make

too many connections. Etc. and excess. I've zombie-
walked through stores with a rotting bank account

and a credit card corpse, pulled the trigger on a
purchase then watched as it was dumped on my

doorstep, dead on arrival. All of these things were
laid to rest before their prime, under a pile of

promises. Before they were able to know the
grace of living without the burden of survival.

I guess everything dies except for capitalism.
Even my mind is an assembly line of temporary

junk. I've been mad at math for going under just
because I'm drowning in earthly temptations. I

have anxieties that shop me around like corporate
parts. Fears that have their place but only live in

closet-like mental spaces, collecting dust until a
new worry entices me with its spotless shine. All

of this stuff will eventually be laid to rest
when I realize I've spent too much time

and money confusing treasure with trash.
I've made room for things that ended up

too heavy on my heart and hands to hold.

KINFOLK

We assume
that rolling over
in a grave
is the only way
our dead kinfolk
express trauma
in the afterlife.

Surely there's
other ways
for ghosts
to let us know
they are disappointed
in the living
and taking notice
of earthside mistakes.

Perhaps they could
gift us with a haunting:

A night terror
in the middle
of a daydream,
or a cool death
chill breath
during meditation.

Rolling over
in a grave
is a silent protest
that never reaches
the oppressor;

it assumes
the repressed
are content
with nothing more
than minor movements
inside rotting spaces,
freely sleeping
in man-made cages.

It also assumes
we are satisfied
with being
walked over,

as grave diggers
take great care
to not disturb
already uncomfortable
bones.

GERRIDAE (SELF PORTRAIT, PART 5)

I'm here to honor all parts of myself:

The man who is scared of death
but romanticizes heaven,

the warrior who would kill for his daughter
then stays up all night spooked by shadows,

the fire-driven miracle seeker
who pretends to rise above everything,

the hot mess.

The punk rocker,

the full-grown gentleman who cries
when watching *Star Wars* cartoons.

A descendent of sassafras drinkers. Of collards,
cabbage, and black-eyed peas in Orangeburg,
South Carolina.

I'm here to honor every version of myself:

The teenager who was too embarrassed
to tell his friends he wrote poetry,

the sour adult who is proud
that his muse has the confidence of honey,

the polymath and the
adrenaline avalanche of youth,

the body that is well on its way to decay,

the empath who water-skips through life
but is afraid to go under.

I'm here to give grace to everything I am:

To lay a blanket next to the grave
of my former selves,

and sit among seeds that were
never meant to flourish,

and dig up reminders of how
I've come to be in bloom.

THIS IS A TRIP

SET & SETTINGS

An intention
becomes a wish
becomes a bloodstream
whisper. A tone that transforms
into a bone-solid conversation with
the body. A voice that's muted in a world
wildly strung out on noise. And it told me:
"It's not the commotion that clogs your mind,
it's the choice you keep making to listen to it."

THE GOSPEL

Consider yourself lucky
if you have
the presence of mind
to remind yourself
of miracles.

We're too farsighted
when looking up
for evidence
of heaven.

Paradise
can be a purely
eye-level
experience.

For example:

My daughter
walks on water
after every storm.

Before the clouds
have had a chance
to make a dry
apology for the mess
they made,

a little girl's feet
find rapture in the
leftover pockets of rain
that overstayed
their welcome.

She's unbothered
by the lingering silver
that hangs around
after a downpour
because

joy doesn't have
to go far
to find a home:

It can be directly
in front of you,
inviting you
to make a splash,

and worship
the gospel
of everyday
things.

STORE-BOUGHT BUDDHA

I've burned
all of the sage,
but I am
barely on fire.

I've counted
every inhale
and exhale of air
and still came up
short of breath.

I've sat in silence
only to unpause
an explosion
of thought.

I've kissed
cold hands,
hoping to come away
with a warm
and friendly touch,

and then I realized

that no amount of incense,
no quiet meditation,
no body
can hold what
makes me whole.

I hope to remember
that the world
needs nothing
from me
but my authenticity
and willingness
to be human

in the moments
when I cannot
conjure
temporary magic.

EARTHQUAKE DANCE

And we opened ourselves up
in a way I hope the earth never does.
Our friendship, solid as concrete,
held fever at its core.

And we were so hot
our energy triggered fire alarms
at every graffiti-stained hole in the wall.
Every rumble of rum
or tremor of tequila
shook us from the inside
and knocked us off our feet.

And we walked into rooms
knowing death
or ecstasy
was one breath away. Not yet
ghosts. Haunting the haunts.

And we were natural disasters,
too hot to touch.
Hard-headed gamblers
flipping a coin
to chase tail.

And we were Goliaths in a holy story
that didn't need any more giants.
I was poetry, promise,
and power trips. Turned on

by every sudden release
of energy, talking my way
in and out of rock-solid aftershocks.

And we were weekend warriors,
temporary residents in our own homes,
paying the price to a liquid landlord
who told us that
heat held inside
cannot stay underground forever.

And it was beautiful.

And somehow
we survived.

IAN

The trees in our neighborhood
started dancing, so we knew that
Mother Nature was about to spin
another devastating tune. Apparently,
the forest can find melodies long before
a song's first note. Meanwhile, I'm sitting
on the floor, building blocks with the
two loves of my life. The window canvas
of our living room blended agitated grays
with the rhythmic green silhouette of branches,
threatening us with a full-blown dance party.

After the jamboree started, the lights went out
and the rowdiness continued. We noticed how
cold & claustrophobic the air can get in a party
like this. We noted how the weather can get stuck
in our heads. I heard the beat of the wind like a
heavy metal drummer. It was so loud that my
ears started hurting. Inside the refrigerator, the
food began its slow fade soiree with decay.
Somehow we slept, and woke up to a silenced
madness. Our neighbors were happy to clean
up the mess. Hungover skies wide open.

DEALATE

Sometimes I am a bird
that is afraid of heights.
And I wonder

if it's the wind
or my wings
that I'm resisting.

Because there are
misty minded mornings
where I can't boost myself

from the ghost hum static
of low frequency thoughts

and I cannot
hover among
anything but

the clouds in my head,
much less get out of bed.

Sometimes my desire
for elevation is as sexy
as the muscle

that spreads feathers out
from a peacock's tail,

but I am unwilling
            to come into
full color transformation

            when the air is
            littered with
            self-made pollution.

Sometimes
            I am in the grace
of the moon's gaze

            and I know its light
            was meant to kiss my back
            as its breath carries me

above rivers, people,
            and predators of worry. But
gravity can be the greatest addiction.

            And I don't know how
            to release my body from it

or soften the blow
when every internal valley
surrenders to the

head-first rush of a fall.

CLOSE
YOUR
EYES
TO
WELCOME
THE
DARK,

THEN
SQUINT
TO
ADJUST
TO
THE
LIGHT
INSIDE.

UNKNOWN

Commissioned for an original opera song cycle by UrbanArias about The Tomb of the Unknown Soldier.

1.

As the morning rises
with the clean air of summer,
my mind is clouded
in smoke.

Anxiety is ammunition
for a duty
that haunts
my dreams:

A war that will
take me away from home,
a departure
that digs deep
within the battlefields
of my soul.

I am one
of many warriors
willing to
fight for a country
that promises freedom,

a country
that I am proud
to call
home.

2.
Home is a hollow space
when worldwide hostility
takes ahold of its habitat.

Beneath this roof
are memories
of life without combat,
a breath before bloodshed,
a love untouched by fear.

I am haunted
more than I am happy.

Reading letters
loaded with the tragedies
of war,
stories about future legends,
soon-to-be ghosts who
fought with honor,

and lost their lives
without losing their faith.

3.
If death has a sound,
then I am now its echo.

Silence will soon
pass through me

and I will remember
that I was made
to have an ending.

And war,
with its infinite reverence,
also has boundary.

I am far
from my family,
but I will soon
be home.

4.
With honor,
I march.

21 steps
in time

for the timeless spirits
of soldiers.

With service,
I march.

21 seconds
in rhythm
for the breathless voices
of the decorated
and departed.

With commitment,
I march.

24 hours
in tempo
to guard the ghosts
who gave their lives
for our country

so that we
can safely call
this land
our home.

5.
Layers of remembrance
hover over us like clouds.

When it rains,
we are wrapped
in sorrow
because we can't escape
the memory of
fallen heroes.

How many storms
have gone unnoticed?

How many more
downpours deserve
our attention?

Our homes
and hearts
are enlivened
by the recognition
of generations
who are gone,
but never forgotten.

A MORNING'S AFTER

It's as if
the rainbows
have forgotten
how to be soft,

and the clouds
lost their color,

or the other way
around.

As if your eyes
need permission
to blink

and a dry mouth
is home
to a muted tongue's
memory of last night's
damp straining.

It's pillow bonding
without asking
the pillow
if it wanted
company.

It's breaking in
the morning
with a bulky brain,
carrying heavy thoughts.

It's the
Saturday morning ash
from Friday night's fire.

It's the firm aftertaste
of too many bourbon
and gingers

and the way the moonlight
paints gray shadows
on the mattress
after the streetlights
absorbed all of your color.

It's getting old

because you
are getting
older.

THE MIRACLE & THE LANDMINE

A poem
is a psalm
is a balm
for the body
and the bone
and the skin.
It's the wind
blowing words
in your ear
when the fear
needs to speak.

A poem
is a song
is a bomb
in your name
when your mind
is a mine
with some frost
holding flame.
It's the sound
that you found
making heat.

LADY PHOENIX

When we met,
I pocketed the warmth
from your fire
before you
blew ash
in my veins.
I now breathe for you
with fevered lungs,
and burn for you
with a firework
tongue.

SOMEONE WILL TELL YOU TO STEP OUTSIDE OF YOUR COMFORT ZONE,

but sometimes you need to be reminded that it's okay to see the beauty of your own boundary. Stay inside and notice the way sunlight cuddles your bed. Call it a spell. Pay attention to the sorcery of a family recipe. Rewind your tongue and refresh its memory. If your heart is heavy, that's okay. Change will not happen today. Close your eyes and forfeit your internal revolutionary war. Be a prisoner to your own style of comfort and, in the process, remember who you are. Water the plants. Lay low in a culture obsessed with rising. You deserve to indulge in self-love and remain faithful to a memory's grace. Go back to where you started. That's where the magic happens.

SOUTH SENSORY

My house is a window-seat movie theater.
Every morning, I can watch geese gather in a
well-choreographed triangle dance with the sky.
Above my head are lights in trapeze, dressed in
wood-flavored earth tones. Below me: The
psychedelic colors of kid toys and their contrast
against white wall corners, cat hair, dirt, and dust.

If these walls could talk, they'd sing a lullaby
of the moon and the morning's birdsong.
They'd speak about the sound of my wife's
gentle hands on piano keys playing "Bluebird."
They'd gossip about my daily communion
with OCD and how I've obsessively organized
and rearranged all of my socks, books, and
records by color.

My home holds stories. Old journal pages
stuck together. Sound memory triggers on cassette
tapes. And the love in our home is addicting.
It's the sweet pancake taste of a fresh fall morning
and mimosas with a splash of gin. It's the
crisp green gifts that come from our garden.
Pumpkin spice muffins and the warmth of
honey infused in just about everything,
including the way we speak to each other.

ALL EARS

I know
enough

to not
talk about

what

I don't
know.

close li

still see

this room, like

wrinkled sheets

d and the dancing

candle ext

dying

103

EFFACE / ERASE (A LETTER TO JONI MITCHELL)

Dear Joni Mitchell,

The first time I was fully aware that you wore blackface on the cover of an album, I tried to take your makeup off with an eraser. When I was younger, I imagined a world where everything was malleable and anyone could take an eraser to paper and remove a layer.

I once destroyed a comic book by trying to scratch off Spider-Man's mask. I wanted to see the fear in his eyes because I'd like all of my superheroes to be vulnerable. I didn't realize it, but at that time I was already aware that it's better to see through the surface of things that present themselves as untouchable.

Anyway, you will always be a hero to me, Joni. But I wish I could unsee that album cover and erase it from my mind.

Because, you know, skin in the wrong hands can be deadly. And I'm tired of my white heroes not understanding their privilege. I'm tired of making excuses for those of us who look the other way when Black and Brown cultures are erased. I'm exhausted from hearing half-assed apologies from white celebrities who wear blackface.

Joni, you still haven't apologized.

I'm tired of putting celebrities on pedestals. And I'm tired of finding out over and over again that racism can't be erased.

But, damn it: I still fan about you like I'm your family. And I don't want to erase your music. *Don Juan's Reckless Daughter* kisses my eardrum with agile bursts of sound and color. *Turbulent Indigo* is a masterclass in metaphor. Even the divisive *Dog Eat Dog* is a brilliant musical detour. Your lyrics are the reason I became a poet.

But Joni, every day someone tweets about you and calls you a racist. They have the right to be angry. I can't erase those words because pixels are more permanent than print.

You are older than me, but I'm old enough to remember when I couldn't even use a brown-faced emoji. I have the right to claim ownership of my skin and question those who appropriate it.

So … you might want to erase this letter. You might

not care what I think. At this moment, you might be writing a new song about the way the sun has a sugar tongue, or how the belly of the world will devour our innocence like honey and eventually shit us out.

That song will be brilliant, because you are a brilliant songwriter.

If only your career was as sweet as people keep saying it is.

Sincerely,

moments when
simply
that
I was
cold

EYE CONTACT

Throw something away
you thought you couldn't
live without. Turn its

memory-triggered touch
into trash. Remind yourself

you have outgrown the past.
Look the future in the eyes &

make it uncomfortable. Keep
diamond recollections on

your mind and wear a crown
then throw the crown away. There

are things you call holy that
are praying to be destroyed.

TUNE UP / TUNE OUT / TUNE IN

I.

The first time I got behind the wheel of a car,
it felt like I had the power of gravity in my hands.
In that moment, I was more than just a

teenager with no destination – I was holding the
electromagnetic force of undiscovered planets.
Steering a 1994 green Chevy Cavalier was a portal

into a universe with infinite range and
possibility, chasing miracles while listening to
carefully constructed mixtapes.

II.

I drove to the grocery store today. Didn't feel the
pull. The world has melted into the ordinary. My
hands have learned to stay in their earthly lane.

My emotional roadmap is on autopilot. The same
paths and the same streets. I'm now handling a body
that has too many miles. Sometimes on the verge of

breaking down. Sometimes too damaged to move.
Nervous in a new way. I'd rather be on my couch
than in a car seat.

III.
I use these same hands to write poems. My pencil has not lost its force of attraction. My notebook is capable of creating galaxies, not just being inside of one.

My muse wanders aimlessly to eventually reveal emotional blind spots. *It always takes me there.* And I'm noticing how the signs on this path say "be aware" instead of "beware."

DEAR DELILAH,

I want you to believe
I am as strong as Samson
every time you lay with me
and unlock the thoughts
that are hidden
beneath layers of tightly woven locs.

I want you to think of me as a lion,
calmly walking through
a forest fire of mystery –
the king of his domain,
the ruler of ash.

I want to be strong enough
for you to ride on my back
and latch on to the muscles
that arch and bend to your body
when we make love.

But Delilah,
it's moments like these
when I gain my strength from you
and the way your hair
looks in the morning,
tangled in my mane,
as you sleep.

It’s you
who finds me in the wild
and brings me back home
when I am weak.

MIXER
out
po12
(drum)
VOLCA keys

THE ACOUSTICS HERE

When you
play my heart

like the harp strings

of Alice Coltrane,

I feel the
glissando on my spine,

and I vibrate between

the notes

as we echo

and endure.

FLUSHED & IN BLOOM (A SPOKEN WORD POEM)

when I was in
the 8th grade
I wore baggy pants
and my book bag
on my chest
because I was not
bold enough to
throw the monkey
off my back.

Inside of
the backpack
was a lack of confidence
weighing me down
I had not found my voice.

This is the portrait
of a Black boy
in bloom-
the Brown-eyed baby
whose birth's purpose
was to unearth poems.

when I was in
the 9th grade
I became brilliant
at being silent,
lost in the soundproof
walls of my mind
trying to find
my voice.

This is the portrait
of a bashful teenager
in bloom -
blind to the way
he was bruising
his inner strength

searching and searching
for a voice.

when I was in
the 10th grade
I ate lunch alone
in the bathroom stall.

I was so shy
that eye contact
clicked a lock
in my throat.

Because of that
it was impossible
to indulge in food
or cook up a conversation
so isolation
had its advantages
and served me well:
I got used to it
and the awkward smell
of a boys bathroom
in the '90s,

the inadequate way
toilet paper impersonates
a napkin,

the sound of Airwalks
squeaking on brown tile
and the way
my mouth,
full of food,
could turn tight-lipped
in a flash,

the ease in which
I could hold my breath
and hide from an
undiscovered abundance,

the disgusting
rubbery chewy meat
of an undercooked hotdog
swimming in an anxious belly.

I was never hungry
for attention;
but I starved for
silence

And I had not
found my voice.

SIDE NOTE:
Raise your hand if
you are frustrated
that your school
didn't offer a class

on how to be
invisible.

I had to learn it
on my own,
and create the
curriculum.

I taught myself
how to quarantine

26 years
before the
pandemic,

26 years
before knowing
that it wasn't.

healthy to walk
around hallways
with an emotional
violence,
going to war
with myself
while carrying
every weapon
I could fit in my palms

before I learned
that making poems
would be the
best kind of bomb.

Because poetry
saved me.

Poetry brought me
back to my core,

poetry blossomed
the boy who didnt
Know he had wings.

Poetry made me sing.

when I was in tune
enough
to write this poem,
I brushed off
any bad feelings.
about myself
because I broke free

from that monkey
on my back
and I unpacked
a beautiful,
booming, blissful
and brave voice.

This is the portrait
of me
now.

THE YOUTH DECAY

Remember the honey-dipped sound of sin, stretched out through smoke-drenched sorrow, where strangers danced to the backbeat of '80s music tickling their hips. Remember how I burned with fire as my hands stayed curved along the icy cold slopes of slippery cocktails. Remember the sound of alarm clocks and grown children scrambling for their mothers, masked in youth and perfumed skin. Remember how you looked at me to see yourself because all of the mirrors were broken and you saw how beautiful you were. Remember the moment you turned your back and I whispered "lust" because I knew you wouldn't hear. Remember the empty conversations that echoed through the scandals taking place in the room next door, down the street, and on cell phones. Remember life as a perfect narrative succumbing to imperfection once the lines begin to blur. Remember the wet sound of truth quenching the thirst of dried-up lovers before eventually bathing in little white lies. I will remember my fingernails on strangers leaving marks on the decay of endless nights.

JUST SAYIN'

A
surefire
way
to
destroy
someone's
mind

is to
give
them
the
option
to
do
so.

THE SPIDER

I remember
when love
was an elusive spider –

an intruder
that kept
trying to creep
into my life,

crawling between the cracks
of hardwood floors
before disappearing
into the shadows
of sleepless
nightmares.

I spent restless years
trapped by distraction,
haunted by
a thing I could not catch,

but secretly wanting
a tarantula
to come, unannounced,
and shake me awake.

When it finally happened,
love sent shivers
up and down
my spine.

It slowly
made its way
from doubt and darkness
into beauty
as I unraveled
out of fear
and willingly walked

into a woman's
web.

CODE.

If I write lines of poems
like I write lines of code,
no comma
would be out of place
and every quotation mark left open
would throw the whole piece off center.

Maybe coding is, in fact,
poetry.

Maybe life is, in fact,
poetry
and we are the result
of a universal code
where X's and O's
are fingers and toes,
the perfect design of
human form.

I define myself
in high definition
after years of
sleepwalking
through a fuzzy dream.

I've turned on computers
to turn off my mind,
I'm unplugging myself
to find a connection.

Where does our
electricity come from?

Maybe the light that's
inside
is designed
to hide our shadows
and we are
wasting our time
placing darkness
where it does not belong.

Maybe at this hour
we should
turn on the power
we are born with
and
search for more
bandwidth
to ignite a
network of our
net worth
and treat people
like poetry –

writing and rewriting code
until all of our history
is recorded.

SMALL TALK

Take off your shoes and slip out of
what you think you know about
us. Despite your persistence, we are
more than just casual conversation.

Shed your skin and slide into
bed with me so we can write poetry.
No paper.

Let's throw words around the dark,
absorb them, then forget about it all
in the morning.

In the daytime, we'll talk about
the weather and wonder whether
our friends can read between the lines.

It will be our little secret.

WATCHING HER SLEEP

Her heartbeat is like a drumbeat
in stereo. Its bassline

underlines my breathing in the
echoes of her bedroom. The

first time I slept there, I
could not conjure dreams. Instead,

I slipped inside the silence
between her rhythm and counted

each grain in the sand of time. I
ran my thoughts through it and

found a song waiting for me
when she opened her eyes.

SKELETAL REMAINS

Charleston,
what does it feel like
to walk on bones
buried under cobblestones,
historical markers
of muted melanin
with unmarked stories
never told?

Casio SK-5, Yamaha DD-1(

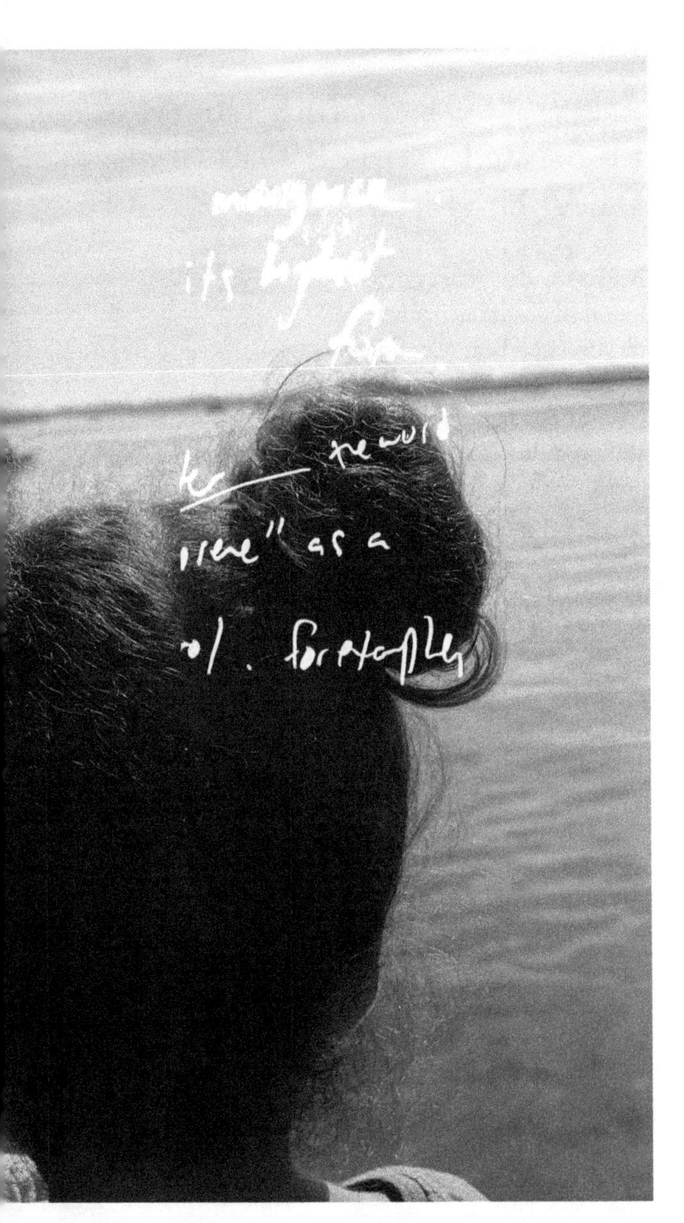

A DOCTOR TELLS US IT'S NOT A LIFE OR DEATH SITUATION

Before my daughter's lungs
found a consistent rhythm,
they were off beat. Coming in

on the one, one, three, two. Unsteady
and unsettled. Too fast, and not
finishing the notes. The nurses

are worried. Concerned
with her cadence. My mother was
once scared for mine because

she found a punk rock CD
on my nightstand. It was a threat.
A kind of music she didn't

understand. A specialist comes
and gives us the notes my daughter
should be playing. He sounds like

sheet music of worry. I tell myself she
is already a fan of Ornette Coleman.
Or Autechre. Imagine that: A baby

who'll skip lullabies for bebop and
experimental electronic music. Instead,
they hook her up like a drum machine,

wires everywhere. Measuring her
beats. One, one, three, two eventually becomes
one, two, three, four. I don't remember

what it was like when my lungs
arrived under water, already expert
swimmers. More fish than flesh. I just

know what it feels like to be a new
parent. In and out of emotional control,
drowning in panic before everything
finds its steady pulse.

BLACK NUMEROLOGY

for Walter Scott

Walter Scott,
I've watched
your death
hundreds of times.

Recently,
I counted
the steps
it took
before the eighth shot
grounded you:
13.

You took
13 paces,
running for
your life,
in line and
online,
the warrior stride
of a 50-year-old
body
that died
too soon.

I wonder
how many
impressions

your feet made
before that
moment.

You probably
walked
hundreds of miles
alive
prior to
poets putting
numbers
on your death march,
countless footsteps
covering the earth
as a son,
a forklift operator,
massage therapist,
father of four.

I wonder
how many
more miles
you would have
walked
holding your
grandchildren.

Would they
have been aware
of the
deep layers
of dark blues
you carried
as a Black man
living in the South?

My mouth
is tired of
sounding out the syllables
it takes to talk
about America's
favorite pastime:

Counting bullets
and burying Brown bodies.

STRANGE ROOTS (THE DIGGING)

I.
Deep down, I know that you can't
take away my shine. It's been perfected
over generations of mining. My ancestors
spent years digging through dirt
for any sign of a gem,

any treasure that can peek
through parasites. But the past
is so dirty and deep-rooted
that sometimes I am too tired
to dig for hope.

II.
Black people are born with brightness
but we can spend our whole lives
navigating a world of shade.

We shine brighter as ghosts.
finding light in death, fire in heaven,
earthly riches with graves
that glow in the dark.

III.
When you dig me under,
I hope that my casket will have
no need for a light bulb,

because my life was full of
so much shining
that death is not a dimming,
but a false shadow.

IV.
Chicago, 2008:
A young white man calls me "nigger"
as I'm walking to a concert.

"Nigger" is a word meant to burn.
It's a tool meant to put you underground
before your grave.

V.
Charleston, 2017:
An older white woman
reminds me
that, to her, I am
nothing but dirt.

VI.
Here I am, again, forced to rise above
worms that are meant to
feed on my soul
and decompose the spirit.

QUEEN

I thought I knew what love *looked* like
when it stood before me
as royalty devoid of diamonds
and emotion robbed of its wealth.

I thought I knew what love *felt* like
as I walked up to its majesty's court,
and ran my fingers against crowns
on dusty statues.

I saw signs of love's treasure
in distant kingdoms,
across roads I couldn't reach
with endless maps
casting silent shadows
on tired feet.

But I never knew what love *sounded* like
until it was whispered in my ear
by a voice whose inflection
was a reflection of our rapture.

Whose birdsong
was the calm of our mornings
spent holding each other
in holy moments,
because love is as near as your next breath
with its arms outstretched.

And its richness,
finally revealed.

SELFIE

Have you ever
taken a photo
of a mountain?

A screen
never quite captures
the magic.

To reduce
a massive,
complex miracle
to pixels is criminal.

It's too simple.

We do the same
to ourselves.

HEARTLINE / BLOODLINE

My grandmother's hands
showed age
like
her heart
showed beauty.

Her voice,
deep and feminine,
wrapped around words
as slow as
the sweat that
found its way down
our forehead on that day,

when she and I
walked together,
arm in arm,
over humid
tombstones
deep into the memory
of our family
and Mother Earth.

Sometimes
I felt like
we were strangers.

Other times,
we were mirrors
of each other.

REFLECTOR

When will I stop
seeing tired eyes
after waking up
next to mirrors?

Why do I call
the cracks on my face
fault lines?

How does the earth
hold so much weight;
so much anxiousness?

When will I stop
messing with my hair?

When will I break free
from vanity's repetition:

Look for natural light. Don't sit with shadows. Suck in your stomach when someone takes a full-bodied picture. Excessive mirrors. Purchase an outfit, return the outfit after trying it on at home. Selfies on the way to the poetry show. Selfies in the car. Adjust brightness. Convince yourself you looked better when you were a kid. Post that photo on social media. Obsessively check for likes. Wipe the grease from your huge forehead. Wipe the shine from your nose. Wipe the photo from your mind. Take another, take another, take another …

How will I not want
to take a photo
of my daughter every day?

How will I not
see perfection
in her complexion
and smooth brown skin tone?

What if someone
says she looks like me?

How will she not be beautiful?

How did I learn
to be okay with
toxic thought?

How do I not
get angry
if someone looks at her
the way I sometimes
look at myself?

THE ARROGANCE OF THE MOON

The moon is unmoving.
Frozen and self-centered
in the atmosphere.
He's proud of the fact
that he can be
steady among a chaos
of satellites
while meditating above clouds
and rubbing elbows with stars.

He's stoic.
Watching egoic people
who are steadily
impressed with excesses,
like high-definition drones
that give us a limited view of the sky,
like phones that run on connections
as stable as tightropes.

Can you hear the moon
laughing at us?

To him, we are
billions of tiny dots
sleepwalking in front
of tinier screens.

Even our dreams
only take us as far
as a data plan.

Who is this man
that we allow to spy on us
like the government?

The all-seeing eye,
peeking through keyholes,
and weaving unwanted light
through windows.

He's wide awake
in the early morning
as we lose our minds
with moonshine.

Look up!

Or better yet, look around you:
Who here thinks they are special?
Who among you doesn't know
how small you are?
Who knows someone
who thinks they can trip the tides?

Who here would love
to hear the conversation
between the sun and the moon
when he decides to eclipse her?

Just like a man:
Arrogant and privileged,
doing everything in his
perched-up patriarchal power
to try and steal a woman's
spotlight.

NOIS
REDU

MAKING LOVE WITH ONLY WORDS

I like how we are
heavy without
tipping the scale.

Beautiful without
makeup and mirrors.

Dancing without
listening to music.

Wanting without
needing.

I like how we
don't need poems
to be poetic.

How you say so much
without speaking,
by just breathing
next to me.

I like how we
learn so much
without knowing.

By just glowing
in the bright spots.

My eyes are closed
and I can see you.

of

ough

thms o

held by the

of ances

the test.

FRANCES & BETTY & CICELY & THE OTHERS

As if the ability to blow into a horn is more important than the ego balloon it took to suck the air out of a woman's voice. As if *Sketches of Spain* is anything but a masterpiece. As if calling yourself "the prince of darkness" is something to be proud of. As if any moonlight could compete with the power light on my CD player the first time I truly understood jazz illumination. As if the only hits some women will remember you by are the ones that were fistprint to skin. As if any rock band could compete with the balls of *Bitches Brew*. As if we are all enablers of dark behavior by not replacing "genius" with "narcissist." As if you weren't a fighter who boxed his way through life and landed every punch. As if you didn't make an impact on every genre in my record collection. As if you never really knew what love was, man.

THE UNITED STATES OF ANXIETY

Welcome to the
United States of Addiction.

In this country,
your smartphone
holds more meaningful moments
than your memory.

Here, social media
is social justice
and history is a hashtag
for broken screens
to get their fix.

Here, fame doesn't
lead to fortune –
just first-world problems.

Echo chambers
for people
at war with themselves.

In the United States of Addiction,
the Declaration of Independence
isn't for independent people –
the quiet-minded
who mind their own business.

In this country,
you can be an activist
by just being active on your phone,
retweeting revolutionary wars,
thumbprints of repetition,
standing up for something
without getting up from your couch,
self-indulgent shouts
with a global view,
but boomerangs of wisdom
from a bedroom in your house.

This is a patriotic poem.

Welcome to the
United States of Anxiety.

In this country,
society tells us
our credit should be straight
while selling us
the crooked path
of commercialism.

Here, citizens take CBD oil
between awkward conversations
and the constant chatter of the mind.

Boredom is not an option
and silence is not sustainable.

In the United States of Anxiety,
Instagram spoons with insomnia.

We swipe up and get out of bed,
wide awake with sleepy minds,
then daydream of FOMO and flat screens –
the American dream.

This is a patriotic poem.

Welcome to the
United States of Assumptions.

In this country,
the color of your skin
allows automatic privilege!

Land, money, power, health,
monuments, legacy, generational wealth …

Here, anything unfamiliar is dangerous,
anyone who disagrees with you
is the devil.

In the United States of Assumptions,
any poet who speaks about injustice

must be an Obama-loving,
hip-hop bumping,
tree-hugging,
emotional heartbeat pumping
soul of a man.

(On the surface,
that may be true about me
but there's many more layers
for you to see …)

Welcome to
the United States of Aggression.

In this country,
we freely walk over broken bones
in the basement of buildings
built by the kidnapped and enslaved.

Here, we walk on beautiful landscapes
and dance on graves.

Welcome to America.
A walking contradiction.

This is a patriotic poem.

MAHOGANY

Who decided to call us "black" and "white"?

When I look at my skin,
I don't see black.
I see Brown.

Brown. Like the color of sand,
a brilliant tan that needs no sun.

Brown, like the mahogany tree bark,
grounded in the summer,
whose green leaves
make the transition into fall,
coffee-stained by the autumn's cool breeze.

Who decided to call us "black" and "white"?

When I look at my wife,
I don't see white.
I see Brown.

Just a lighter shade
than mine.

Brown is the cinnamon
that colors her iris.

Brown are the arms
that wrap around me
during a bronze sunset.

Brown are the layered bricks
of our home's foundation.

Who decided to call us "black" and "white"?

When I look at all of you,
I see shades of Brown.
A sea of one color.

Ripples of love
floating along a sea change.

There are so many words used to *divide* us.
To fool us into seeing ourselves
through foggy lenses.

We are more
than a box-checked statistic,
we are more
than a census.

I am not
black and white.

I am awake.

THE AMERICA I KNOW COULD USE A GOOD CRY

I met America at a neighborhood bar.

He offered me a shot of rum and I reminded
him that Captain Morgan was a slave owner,
so the bartender awkwardly slipped another
liquid lie down my throat. I ordered another drink
and was channeled by dark spirits. The courage of
Black ghosts who haunt American dreams.

I told him I loved him and I wanted him to sleep
well. "But I know I've been in your nightmares,"
I said. "I want to be your friend, but only if it's a
deep relationship. Only if you show me that you
are not scared of your baggage. Bring your whole
history to the table."

America cracked open another beer as a tear ran
down his face. He said,

"I was born in a house not my own, and my
fathers demanded that their portraits hang on
every wall. White paint covers each brown brick
and our backyard is a museum of unmarked
graves."

"Despite this, a garden grows," I said. "And
every home can be torn down and rebuilt again."
"But I've been told I shouldn't completely let you

in," he said. "Some people in my family stand in the doorway, blocking the entrance."

He left before I could tell him that my people have a history of finding ways inside broken spaces and making them whole again.

20 'TIL INFINITY

Look at us!
Footsteps making echo sounds
on sidewalks.
Black men leaning in for a head nod
instead of a handshake.
Loneliness as survival.
Curbside cocktails.
Men in masks
walking pit bulls.
Parents loving
and loathing
school shutdowns.
Cigarette smoke dancing
around silent porch
g a t h e r i n g s .
Physical and emotional
distance. Paranoia,
as in
"can the trees spread disease?"
Ghost streets.
Some of us
taking slow breath
in the middle of
fast ration.
Dark mode option
of the internet.
Moms with strollers,
coffee and cellular phones.
Bicyclists letting us in

on the mid day sun secret.
Still finding time to
put on lipstick.
Mind and body going in circles,
off balance.
Prayers up
through pollution.
Janet Jackson
in headphones
sampling Joni Mitchell's
big truth chorus.
This is how we chill
from 2020 'til.

HOW TO READ A BOOK

Dust off the cover
and wipe your hands
on a shirt.

Focus your eyes
on the image
then peel back the first page.

Look at the title,
and the way
the author
stamps a story with subtitles and

chapters that weigh down
the spine like years
weighing down our spines then

wrinkling the skin.

We are just characters
trapped by our own plots.

But every way we angle the book,
the story
remains the same.

HOPE IS IN THE LISTENING

Official 2020 Charleston Mayoral Inauguration poem

City as sorcerer and storyteller, sharp-eyed
observant, holy grandmother. She's survived 350 years

because the longevity of the Lowcountry requires
a special kind of magic. Today, we are witnesses

to that witchcraft. Citizens of its charm. Today,
she is the voice connecting her family: The tourist

and tour guide, cradling history in their arms
like a crying infant. The LGBTQ+ community,

joyous and resilient in the shadow of hate crimes.
Plantation workers sending one-way postcards

to ghosts. Black poets, the great interpreters
of Southern truth. The farmer, hand-delivering

homegrown sunshine. The mayor, whose job is to
see hope through floods and watered-down politics.

Charleston's story should be defined by
this diversity. The sounds of promise and protest.

She may be old, but her best days are ahead.
Whatever challenges await, we will face them together

because she hears us, people of change.
She hears us.

THE RUNNING RIVER

The river never broke a sweat.
It went for miles around us,
running in place
in search of a silent moon.
The darkness was her perfect partner,
leading them all
to the finish line,
where the morning
threw its hands up
as the winner of the race.
We stood on the sidelines,
rooting for time to suspend us,
staring down the clock
and knowing this was
not the end,
but the beginning of our journey
toward forever.

THE PULSE (A POEM ABOUT CHARLESTON)

We live in Charleston!

Where the sidewalks scream
on Saturday nights
and the corners rotate
budding musicians
with skin-tight dreams,

where strings of pearls
search for salvation
then sweat out their frustrations
on the backs of rooftops,

where the homeless sprout
like weeds through concrete
seeking two dollars, a handshake
and a little bit of sunshine,

where the humidity
chokes you out of your breath
but you still manage to speak to the
spit-shine waiters
who serve $95 bottles of wine,

where two blocks away,
a $5 pitcher of liquid gold
spills on the canvas of sticky floors,

where love lingers on cobblestone streets
in narrow alleyways,
but the smell of sex
is the foundation
for first and last impressions.

We live in Charleston!

Where shadows are surrounded
by the ocean
and sea-seeing people gasp for air
from knee-deep bills
and dirt-cheap thrills,

where those with
no sense of history's melody
sync with the songs of the city's slaves,

where the poets scrape stanzas
off of streetlights
and if they scream loud enough
maybe someone won't be afraid of the dark.

I live in Charleston!

Where church steeples and cranes
look over us

and multicolored houses
house live-in servants,
where fast-rising hotels
rise above slow-moving clouds
that cast floods on the corner
of America Street,

where parades of one color
get one day to celebrate
then hide in the shadows
of gentrification,

where Gullah cuisine
is too expensive
for Gullah people.

The Holy City!

Where the steady beat of jazz
is the beat of our streets
and the dialect of our past
writes future conversations,

where bridges and bike lanes
break bread with politics,
while some of us preach peace
with uneducated tongues.

Where the Angel Oak tree is young
compared to our vanity,
where $16 burgers
are sold in the middle of a food desert
while every community
wants a piece of the pie.

Where grandmothers sit on porches,
watching us change
while the problems of our city
remain the same.

We live in Charleston!

Where the ghosts and yoga studios
call themselves "holy"
and the vintage market calls itself "holy"
and the whiskey drinkers go to church
to feel tender and holy,

where potholes and potheads
blow smoke through steam-filled summers,
and the pandemic was brushed away
like palmetto bugs laughing in the face of death.

Where some of us dream
of an underground scene

to hold on to the spirit of elevation,

where halter tops don't stop in the winter
for people with disposable incomes
and opposable thumbs.

The Holy City.

Where the hurricanes are coming,
where the hurricanes are coming,
where the hurricanes are coming.

Another Charleston is being built
above our heads.

Maybe this one won't flood?

he way
he microphone.
sed to think
needed a power chord
be turned on,
used to obsess,
the dust
t scratches my throat,
used to not know
t my noise I make
pure human sound
I am not a broken
record.

BLACK CLOTH

For the Emanuel 9

Racism,
let us no longer walk in your shoes.
You are a traveler of darkness,
a walker of shadows,
cloaking yourself in a black cloth
like the grim reaper
and arming your soul
with the tools of a terrorist –
a misguided soldier
who's trying to start a war.

My sisters,
heaven was as close as your breath
that night.
You came to Mother Emanuel
to worship in the glow of God,
and speak the light that flows from love.
How beautiful of Him to hear your words
and lift you into the arms of Christ.

My brothers,
you walked toward heaven with focus,
even when your shoes were stained
with the dirt of intolerance.
A black cloth lays silent
at Clementa Pinckney's seat,
resting under a single rose.
It was taken from our city's soil,
where seeds of faith continue to grow.

Charleston,
I see heaven in your tears
and feel the weight of sadness
in your voice. I've seen strangers
hold hands as the sun wraps us
in unbearable heat,
I've watched children of contradiction
come together for the unity
of the Holy City.

But South Carolina,
nine more members of your family
are now in heaven
and you have to confront
the reality of racism,
the dusk of pain, the lightlessness
of the dawn.

And I would rather hang a black cloth
on a flag pole
than give the confederate flag
another glimpse of the sun.

ered

is not

interact

sound, and the

n to silence

who can hear

's my

build a

the quiet.

WHEN I'M AT HOME, I WATCH *STAR WARS*. WHEN I WATCH *STAR WARS*, I WRITE HAIKUS ABOUT WAR, VIOLENCE, AND MEMORY.

Episode 1
Battle droid theory:
Turn war into fetish, make
army of robots.

Episode 2
Soldiers are now slaves
in galaxies of mass graves,
programmed for violence.

Episode 3
Fear is mutation,
soul transformation and sin
when man starts to kill.

Episode 4
The family back home:
Echoes and faint memories
of life before war.

Episode 5
Too dark, now. Mind filled
with trauma and torture. Mask
for the suffering.

Episode 6
Confront the demon.
Put end to internal war.
Make peace before death.

Episode 7
A ghost's memory
haunts the new generation
and passes down pain.

Episode 8
Young resistant minds
have the spark to start over.
Reclaim history.

Episode 9
If demon returns,
reprogram memory, and
write your own story.

"SLEEP WHEN THE BABY SLEEPS,"

they always say.

As if sleeping
is a switch
easily turned on.

Especially when
all of your
mind's power
is being used
for the electricity
of fatherhood.

Especially when
you know that
a dad could be a God,
but you are
a feminist.

Especially when
your daughter's breathing
could brush the quiet
off of a cloud,

but you keep checking
for storms
through weather-worn
insomnia.

What if a baby
is a poem?

*Ask me to sleep
through that.*

Where every breath
is a mirror fog
writing itself
through unstable,
forgetful darkness
and each mind twitch
is a pen stroke.

No matter
what happens,

the words
will be written,
a mouth
will be fed,
a woman
will be born,
a person
will be an echo

and your eyelids
will be heavy
with daylight.

THE NEW FOUNDATION

Every moment that you are alive
is the only moment that matters.
The past is a glass house
and we throw stones
trying to shatter walls
that need to come down.

We are all architects of negativity –
brick by brick of bold thoughts
holding together
bodies bound by blood
but burned by love,
so we let bugs into our house.

And each infestation
is a manifestation
of our own insecurity
until the walls come down.

Be aware of the model you are building.
Allow enough room for God.
Give Jesus the floor plan.

Let Buddha have a spare key
so that He
may open up the blinds
when you are blind
to your own light.
Let your home be a haven for heaven

but dig deep
if the walls need to come down.

People are insane,
living like zombies –
blindly walking,
even *stalking* themselves,
staring at computer screens
that poison their pockets,
claiming the key to a connection
is really an infection of the mind.

We are born with the breath of rhythm,
yet we cut the cords of our connections
and we find ourselves
stuck between the intersection
of freedom and ego.

But which way will you go
when your walls come down?

I am not perfect:

I have been known to cling to clutter
and sit comfortable in uncomfortable chairs.
I have been known to obsess over obsessiveness.
I have been known to keep friendships
when they do nothing but harm.

What about you?

Do you sound an alarm
when your foundation is on fire?
Or do you fan the flames
long enough for five o'clock to roll around?

Well, this is not happy hour.

This is the time for time
to not be spent
counting down eight hours
behind the desk
of your own shadow.

This is the time to
free yourself from the mental cage
where all ages grow to know pain,

This is the time
to start a new revolution –
where love is the solution
to the troubles of the world,
with weapons of mass reconstruction,
rebuilding houses whose walls
need to come down.

silence becomes an instrument for spoken word soundscapes.
simply walk.

THE LANGUAGE WE LEARN

I.

Masculinity
doesn't have
to be toxic,
but some men
choose to put
poison
on their
tongue.

Foaming
at the mouth
before flinging
unholy thoughts
into action.

Hungry for prey,
licking their lips
as biting words
draw blood.

Women do nothing
to feed
this venom.

Porn and
pop culture
evolved
from paper cuts

to pixels
as men
learned
negative language
and spread it around
like a virus.

II.
The first time
I put poison
on my tongue,
I did not
notice
the taste.

The shared language
of youth
stuck
to the roof
of my mouth.

It was the
bad breath
of boys around me,
leaving an
aroma of adolescence,
ignoring the lessons
of our mothers.

III.
The men
that I know
are repulsed
by the taste
of poison.

We are hungry
for clarification
over contamination,

adjectives
that no longer
melt from objects
to people.

Simply put,
we've freed
ourselves
from the pollution
of the mind.

But,
to all of the women
who have been sexualized,
we apologize.

To all of the women
I have sexualized,

I apologize.

(AT THE ROOT IS RESTLESSNESS)

Am I

an

echo

of God

enough

or

am I

an

ego,

just good

enough?

LOVE

Jordan: The best decision I ever made was to marry you. Thank you for being my lifelong lover and partner. Thank you for being you.

Rei: You have my whole heart. You've taught Jordan and I so much in your three years. I'm extremely grateful for your presence and the color that you've brought into our lives.

Love to Betty & Willie Amaker. Love to all of my family and friends. I'm forever grateful for you. And you, too, Mr. Wu.

ACKNOWLEDGEMENTS

American Poets Magazine: "A Doctor Tells Us It's Not a Life or Death Situation"

Academy of American Poets (poets.org): "Give Yourself Some Flowers," "The America I Know Could Use a Good Cry," "A Doctor Tells Us It's Not a Life or Death Situation"

Button Poetry (video contest): "Give Yourself Some Flowers"

Charleston City Paper: "The Word 'Supreme' Has Been Canceled," "Black Cloth," "They / Them / Us"

The Citadel: "Honor Code (Embers)"

City of Charleston: "Hope is in the Listening"

Jasper Project: "Gerridae," "Bacteria"

The first poem. Written in 1991.

written by: Marcus Angkler

In My Room

I'm sitting in my room
thinking of you.
I'm lying on my back
trying to figure what to do.

I love you so much,
it's hard to explain
I think you're the best.
Don't ever change.

Whenever you're around,
I don't know what to say.
The only thing I wish
Is that you'll never go away.

You make my life perfect
when I see your beautiful smile
I can sense your presence
even from a mile.

I'm sitting in my room
in complete darkness.
Wanting to touch your hair,
wanting to caress.

MEET MARCUS

Marcus Amaker (he/him) is a husband, a dad, a son, a music nerd, and a *Star Wars* obsessive. He served as the first Poet Laureate of Charleston, South Carolina, from 2016–22. In 2021, he became an Academy of American Poets fellow. This is his tenth book.

He's also a prolific performer, the award-winning graphic designer of a roots music journal (*No Depression*), a musician, an opera librettist, the creator of a poetry festival, a teaching artist, and an advocate for youth poets.

His work has been recognized by *The Washington Post*, The Kennedy Center, *American Poets Magazine*, Chicago Opera Theater, The Portland Opera, Button Poetry, NPR, *The Chicago Tribune*, Edutopia, *Town & Country*, *PBS NewsHour*, South Carolina Public Radio, *Charleston Magazine*, *Charleston City Paper*, *Post and Courier*, and more. In 2019, he received a Governor's Arts award in South Carolina and was named the artist-in-residence of the Gaillard Center, a world-renowned performance and education venue.

His poetry was used by the Washington National Opera for its Presidential Inauguration Day Concert in 2021, and has been studied in classrooms around the country.

In addition to more than 40 electronic music albums, Marcus has recorded three albums with Grammy Award-winning drummer and producer Quentin E. Baxter. His poem "The Rain" is on two Grammy-nominated albums. He also created a publishing company to release poetry books and host events for poets in his community. June 3, 2021, was named "Marcus Amaker Day" by John Tecklenburg, mayor of Charleston, SC.

He lives in North Charleston, SC, with his wife, their daughter, and a cat named after Wu-Tang Clan.

Printed in the USA
CPSIA information can be obtained
at www.ICGtesting.com
JSHW012354150923
48206JS00001B/1